Tamaskan Dog

Fun Information You Should Know About Tamaskan Dog

Copyright © 2021

All rights reserved.

DEDICATION

The author and publisher have provided this e-book to you for your personal use only. You may not make this e-book publicly available in any way. Copyright infringement is against the law. If you believe the copy of this e-book you are reading infringes on the author's copyright, please notify the publisher at: https://us.macmillan.com/piracy

Tamaskan Dog

Contents

Tamaskan Dog 1
Origin 3
Pedigree 5
Food/Diet 7
Training 9
Weight 11
Temperament/Behavior 12
Common Health Problems 14
Recognized Clubs 15
Coat 16
Puppies 17
Tamaskan Frequently Asked Questions 18
All You Need To Know About The Finnish Wolfdog 23
Amazing Facts About The Tamaskan Wolfdog 37

Tamaskan Dog

Some folks want a dog that looks like a doll, the type that can fit in a purse and feel like an accessory. Other people want something more from their dog. They're seeking a pet that looks like a tamed wolf. Different strokes, as they say! For those dog owners on the hunt for a big boy who looks like he could star in a White Fang remake, may we humbly recommend the Tamaskan.

The Tamaskan may look like a wolf, but this breed is all dog. In fact,

Tamaskan Dog

this pooch was selectively bred by dog breeders in order to create this wolf-like of appearance and they are truly stunning. Tamaskan dogs are both a new and rare breed but they are extremely intelligent and highly versatile in terms of dog sports and working ability. This breed is best for experienced dog owners who have the time and the ability to provide plenty of exercise and mental stimulation.

This isn't a pet for first time dog owners. These pups require work, attention, and care. Yet, the results are clearly worth it for veteran dog owners. So, is the Tamaskan the right doggo to bring into your home? Fortunately, you've come to the right place to find out. Keep your eyes glued to this page and scroll away. Everything that needs to be known about owning a Tamaskan will be revealed below.

Origin

The Tamaskan dog is a fairly new breed, having only been developed in the 1980s. The origins of the breed can be traced back to a group of five Husky-type dogs that were imported into the United States during the 1980s. These dogs were crossed with Siberian Huskies, Alaskan Malamutes, and German Shepherds to create new breed that would resemble wolf in its appearance, while displaying the obedience and intelligence that are characteristic of domesticated dogs. The breed was then exported to Finland for additional development. The first result was the Utonagan dog, but some believe that further crossing of this breed with the Czechoslovakian Wolfdog is what made the Tamaskan dog as we know it today. Unfortunately, we can't be certain of this pup's specific history because like all designer dogs, there simply wasn't much documented.

The purpose for creating this dog breed was to develop a domestic dog that had a wild appearance and strong working ability. It's safe to say that the breeders achieved this goal with the Tamaskan. This dog delivers as advertised. The first litter of Tamaskan puppies came to

Tamaskan Dog

the United States in 2005 and there are now several Tamaskan breeders across the U.S.

Pedigree

The Tamaskan dog was selectively bred from Husky-type dogs that were imported into the USA during the 1980s. The breed was developed with influence from Siberian Huskies, Alaskan Malamutes ,German Shepherd and even a little bit of Czechoslovakian Wolfdog.

While most of these breeds were selected primarily for their wolf-like appearance, the lupine look is not the only goal breeders wanted to achieve with the Tamaskan. Owing to its parents, these hybrids are intelligent, capable, brave, and loyal to their owners. This particular combination of traits (and breeds in their family tree) makes the Tamaskan ideally suited as a companion, working dog, or a family pet. It takes a special animal that can do everything the Tamaskan offers and this pup qualifies as a special achievement in designer dog breeding.

Food/Diet

Because the Tamaskan dog is such a high-energy working breed, these dogs need a commercial dog food diet that is dense in both nutrients and calories. So, choose a high-quality commercial dog food diet for the Tamaskan and consider an active or working breed formula for the best results. Additionally, you should choose kibble that's suitable for your pet's age (puppy, adult, or senior). Your pup's needs will change as he ages just like you, so it's important to find a food that is well suited to your dog's specific stage of life.

If you are ever concerned about establishing or altering your dog's diet, it's always wise to consult with your veterinarian. While dog food manufacturers and pet blogs provide useful feeding guides, they are still guidelines and not gospel. All dogs are different and only your vet is qualified to determine the specific dietary needs of your personal pooch. So always check in with your vet before making any changes to what you put in your dog's bowl at feeding time.

Tamaskan Dog

Because Tamaskans are a highly intelligent breed, they generally respond well to training.

Training

Because the Tamaskan dog is a highly intelligent breed these dogs generally respond well to training. Early socialization and training is essential for this breed to help keep its energy under control. These dogs sometimes develop a stubborn streak so you will need to maintain a firm and consistent hand in training, providing the dog with strong leadership. Newbie dog owners or first-time dog owners might find these impressive dogs too much work, so it's best not to consider this breed if you don't have previous training and ownership experience. Patience and persistence will be vital to successfully training a Tamaskan and not all dog owners are up to the task. It isn't easy, but it's worth it.

With a smart and energetic dog like the Tamaskan, it's best to have a confident approach and rely on positive reinforcement methods. Be consistent and assert yourself as the pack leader, but still use treats and praise as a form of motivation, rather than being harsh or cruel to your new pet. Not only that aversive training is inhumane, but it is also completely ineffective. You'll never get the results you seek by being overly negative while training your pup. It takes a gentle, yet firm hand to properly train a Tamaskan and that's why so few dog owners are truly up to the task.

In addition to basic obedience, housebreaking, and early socialization, you can work with the Tamaskan on more complex learning tasks. This breed does well as a working breed and he excels in various dog sports including obedience, agility, and field trials. Tamaskans love to work and it's amazing what they can accomplish when properly trained.

Weight

The Tamaskan dog is a medium-to-large sized breed that looks similar to the Siberian Husky but it has a stronger build. These dogs typically weigh between 55 and 88 pounds and they stand between 24 and 28 inches tall at the shoulder. In other words, this is a big boy. You won't ever be surprised when one of these dogs walks into a room. They have quite an imposing presence. It's part of the appeal.

Temperament/Behavior

Despite its wild appearance, the Tamaskan dog is actually quite a gentle breed. Sweet and affectionate, they will do well as family pets or companions to singles. They get very attached to their owner and form a very strong bond to their family. Tamaskans won't tolerate being left alone for long periods of time. They are prone to developing separation anxiety. In addition to being very devoted to their closest humans, these dogs are also very friendly and generally have an extroverted personality. All things considered, it's safe to say that this breed likes to be around people and they tend to get along well with children.

Don't forget that these dogs are intelligent and active. As a result, they do require a good deal of exercise as well as mental stimulation to prevent boredom (which can lead to the development of problem behaviors). They need owners who can keep up with their physical and mental needs to thrive. As a working dog breed, they tend to be at their best when they have a task, so consider training them for one of the popular dog sports as an alternative. Something like agility, canine freestyle, pulling, mushing, or flyball. There are plenty of fun activities your Tamaskan could excel at! It's all up to you.

Common Health Problems

Because the Tamaskan is a fairly new breed there is limited information regarding congenital health problems. However, this hybrid was developed from several breeds that are known for good health. So you can expect the Tamaskan dog to be fairly healthy as well. There are, however, a few conditions to which this breed may be prone including cryptorchidism, epilepsy, hip dysplasia, and degenerative myelopathy. As always, it's important to maintain regularly scheduled checkups with a vet (especially as the dog ages) to ensure that any potential health issues are identified and treated as early as possible.

Recognized Clubs

Because the breed is still new, it has not yet been accepted by the American Kennel Club or The Kennel Club in the U.K. It is, however, recognized by the American Canine Association, the Dog Registry of America, and the Tamaskan Dog Register.

Coat

The coat is what gives the breed its wolf-like appearance. These dogs resemble grey Timber Wolves, having a multicolored coat made up of various shades of gray and brown as well as black and white. The Tamaskan dog's coat is double and thick, the tail bushy and straight. This breed exhibits three main colorations: Red Grey, Wolf Grey, and Black Grey.

When it comes to grooming, the Tamaskan is not high-maintenance. A weekly brush will be all it takes to keep their lupine-like fur looking its best. However, these dogs will go through moulting season twice a year and will shed more during this period. To make it more manageable for you and your pet, you'll have to brush them every day during this period. Trust us, the extra effort is worth it.

Puppies

The first litter of Tamaskan puppies was brought to the U.S. in 2005 and they had their own litter in 2007. The average litter size for this breed is between 6 to 10 puppies. Since this is a new and fairly rare breed with attractive looks and desirable personality traits, it might not be easy to find a puppy right away. For Tamaskan puppies, there are usually waiting lists and their price is around $2,000.

But once you get your wolf-lookalike puppy, you'll see it was worth the effort. To make sure your new pet grow into an impressive canine it has the potential to be, make sure to start working with them right away. Tamaskan puppies require a great deal of socialization and training starting early on in their lives and they generally take to training quickly.

Tamaskan Frequently Asked Questions

How much does a Tamaskan dog cost?

A Tamaskan puppy will cost you anywhere between $1,200 and $2,500. There are not many reputable, registered Tamaskan breeders out there, and the price will depend from state to state, as well as on the puppy itself: if the puppy comes already trained and checked by a vet, it will raise the price.

Are Tamaskan dogs good pets?

Tamaskan dogs might look like they belong in the wild, but they have a sweet, kind soul and a great temperament. They are very affectionate and tend to form an unbreakable bond with their humans, so they will truly become your best friend and most loyal companion.

Are Tamaskan dogs aggressive?

Many people mistakenly think that Tamaskan dogs are aggressive due to their wild appearance, but this breed is actually very sweet and loving by nature. Of course, if the dog has been neglected, mistreated, or hasn't gone through basic socialization and training, they can develop behavioral issues the same as any other dog breed.

Do Tamaskan dogs have wolf in them?

Looks can be deceiving- Tamaskan was bred to look like a wolf, but doesn't actually have any wolf in its lineage. Tamaskan dogs have been selectively bred from Husky-type dogs that resemble wolves, without any involvement from wild animals.

Do Tamaskan dogs need a lot of exercise?

Tamaskan dogs are a working breed so they do need a lot of exercise to stay happy and healthy. They are highly intelligent and fairly energetic, so they will need to be mentally and physically stimulated to thrive. Dog sports are a great way to burn off extra energy and build your relationship with your pet, but long walks, hikes, and plenty of fetch in the dog park will do just fine, too.

Are Tamaskans easy to train?

Tamaskans are in no way beginner-friendly dogs, and the same goes for training. These dogs are very smart, and while this means that they will take to training, it also means that they can develop a stubborn streak and make the process more difficult for the inexperienced dog owner. However, with patience, persistence, and positive reinforcement methods, you can achieve great training results with your Tamaskan.

Are Tamaskans protective?

These dogs are very loyal to their families, and, as such, can become very protective of their humans. This doesn't mean that they will make good guard dogs: they are generally friendly and tend not to bark too much, so if you need a watchdog to alert you of intruders, Tamaskan shouldn't be your top choice.

Are Tamaskans good with small dogs?

While a lot will depend on the individual dog, Tamaskans are generally good with other dogs. If the dogs are too small, such as a toy breed, there might be room for trouble, as they might see them as prey. With early socialization, though, there shouldn't be any issues.

Are Tamaskans good family dogs?

Loyal, loving, and friendly, Tamaskan make good family dogs when socialized and trained early in life. They like children and get along well with them, and can grow to be very protective of kids in the family. Similarly, they can be a great family pet for active couples, too, as Tamaskans will love to be included and will form a strong bond with their owners.

Are Tamaskan dogs good with cats?

Tamaskans have a high prey drive, and as such are not recommended for families with cats. While a dog can be socialized to get along with a feline companion, a prey drive tends to manifest sometime later in life and it can really become an issue as your dog will start chasing like crazy for your kitty and maybe even try to hurt her.

All You Need To Know About The Finnish Wolfdog

The Tamaskan, meaning "mighty wolf" in Munsee, is an athletic and cuddly dog breed known as the Tamaskan Husky or the Tam.

Despite this breed's astounding resemblance to the wild wolf, it is all dog.

A Tamaskan dog laying on the snow

Tamaskan Dog

Breeders carefully selected domesticated canines to create the Tamaskan dog's wolf-like appearance. Besides that, this article will cover everything else you need to know about Tamaskan dogs.

What is a Tamaskan Dog?

The Tamaskan dog breed originated in the 1980s to develop a canine with the wolf's appearance, a working dog's drive, and intelligence, but with a house pet's temperament.

This is the goal of the breeders from Finland, Canada, and the United States.

Besides Northern Inuit and other select breeds, only a few dogs resemble wolves.

So, founded in 1988, the breed club imported five Husky-type dogs from the US to the UK that were then bred to the Alaskan

Tamaskan Dog

Malamute, Siberian Husky, and German Shepherd.

As a result of this breeding program, the Utonagan Dog was born.

Despite this success, breeders thought that there was not enough diversity in their collection. To improve its bloodline, they exported the breed to Finland for additional development.

Some believe that breeders further included the Czechoslovakian Wolfdog, making the Tamaskan dog we know today.

There's also some debate that Finnish Origin Huskies have been bred into the Tamaskan bloodline.

It was 2002 when breeders produced the first litter of Tamaskan puppies.

Tamaskan Dog

At that time, it's normal to see one litter of puppies with entirely different features as there was no standardized breed profile or breeding stock. The name Tamaskan didn't even exist back then.

But in 2006, The Tamaskan Dog Registry was founded, naming this new breed the Tamaskan dogs.

From the 21st century, breeders started working together to create litters with a consistent appearance and temperament.

Tams are considered "designer dogs" due to the breed's careful and selective crossbreeding program with purebred bloodlines.

For this reason, the American Kennel Club (AKC) does NOT recognize the Tamaskan breed.

But, the following organizations recognize this breed:

- TDR = The Tamaskan Dog Register
- ACA = American Canine Association
- DRA = Dog Registry of America, Inc.
- APRI = American Pet Registry, Inc.

Taking Care of Your Tamaskan Dog

Tamaskan dogs loves to hang out in the snowfield

Two Tamaskan dogs loves to hang out in the snowfield – Image source

Tamaskans are a low-maintenance dog breed requiring little in the way of grooming. As long as you get them their regular exercise and nutritional needs, you'll have a happy and healthy wolf-like pooch.

Their thick double coats make them better off in moderate to cold weather.

How much exercise do Tamaskan Dogs need?

Because they're related to amazing working dogs and sled dogs, you can expect Tams to have high energy levels, and having 60 to 90 minutes of exercise daily is non-negotiable.

If you're going to let your puppy spend it all on running or jogging, at least 18 miles per week would be sufficient for this canine.

If you have a pool or live somewhere near a lake or beach, you can also take your Tamaskan dog swimming.

Other than that, they need a spacious, fenced-in yard to ensure that Tams can run or play on their own without escaping or running after a cat or a squirrel.

Intelligent breeds like the Tamaskan also require mental stimulation. Think of activities that would make him think and keep him from getting bored.

You can use an interactive toy, do a hide-and-go-seek treats game, fetch, or let him help with errands.

Want to take it up a notch? Tams are also versatile doggos that excel at different canine sports, too.

You can sign your pup in field, agility, or obedience trials. There's also flyball, mushing, canine freestyle, and many more! You and your fur baby won't run out of activities to do.

Grooming: Are Tamaskan Dogs hypoallergenic?

Tamaskans are moderate shedders and NOT hypoallergenic, so consider your allergies before buying or adopting one.

But, they're easy to groom, and you only need to brush them once a week for the majority of the year.

Be aware, however, that Tamaskans are molting their hair bi-annually, meaning they shed more than usual.

During this time, it's best to brush them daily during this period, but they barely cleared the rest of the year.

Due to Tams' repellant double coats, you should only bathe them if they get dirty or muddy. Their coats will keep them from getting smelly unless they get wet.

To keep ear infections away, clean your dog's ears once a week with some damp cotton. Then, dry them out with a clean cloth.

If drooling is a dealbreaker for you, the Tam may not be the best breed of dog for you. They do drool a bit, but not as much as the Basset Hound.

Tamaskan Dog Breeders

Ensure that you're buying a healthy puppy from a reputable breeder by asking for certification, and of course, by doing your research.

The certificate is proof that the dog meets ethical breeding standards and regulations and has undergone health screening for hereditary conditions.

The Tamaskan Dog Register (TDR), the official international organization for Tamaskan breeds, lists various registered Tam breeders.

Tamaskan Dogs for Adoption

It may be even more challenging to find a Tamaskan rescue than Tamaskan dog puppies for sale, as serious fanciers and breeders usually own these designer dogs.

We found this Facebook page for Tamaskan Rescues, and this Tamaskan Dog Rescue is based in the UK.

Tamaskan Dog Compared to Similar Canines

Tamaskans have notable differences from their wolfdog cousins due to the selective breeding program developed in the 1980s. We've broken down some of the key differences below.

Alaskan Malamute VS. Tamaskan Dog

Tamaskan Dog

Alaskan Malamutes are friendly dogs too, but the Tamaskan beats it out in terms of playfulness – with kids in particular.

Also known as Mals, this breed also has more rigorous grooming needs than the low-maintenance Tams.

Siberian Husky VS Tamaskan dog

Siberian Huskies have fewer health conditions than those Tamaskans suffer from, although Tamaskans have longer lifespans. Siberian Huskies have much smaller litters, with only 4 to 8 puppies.

Who should get a Tamaskan Dog?

Tamaskan Dog

As gentle as they are, we do NOT recommend Tams for first-time dog owners.

They require a lot of attention and can't be left alone much, which poses a constantly for people who are always working or love to travel.

Tamaskan Dog

Their intelligence does make them susceptible to training, yet they need an owner who's present and dedicated to a strict discipline regimen every day.

A significant pro in favor of the Tam breed is their lively demeanor with children and peaceful nature, making them great additions to family households.

If you have the time to invest in caring for a Tamaskan dog, you'll have a loyal and devoted companion for life.

Amazing Facts About The Tamaskan Wolfdog

The Tamaskan Dog, also known as the Tam, is a breed of dog that has been selectively bred to look like a wolf dog.

These wolf-like dogs are not purebred as they are crossbred with many other dog breeds including the:

- Siberian Husky

Tamaskan Dog

- German Shepherd
- Alaskan Malamute

There is also some debate about other dog breeds that have been bred into the black grey, red-grey, or wolf grey coated bloodline. Some have speculated the following two breeds of dog too:

- Czechoslovakian Wolfdog
- Finnish Origin Huskies

Although there are many Wolfdogs, these Tamaskan dogs are distinctly separate, a unique breed with their own fanbase and breed association.

Growing in popularity since the 1980s, more questions are starting to be asked about these wonderful Tamaskan wolf dogs.

Tamaskan Dog

But what is there to know about these incredible wolf-like dogs? This article contains seven must-know facts about the Tamaskan dog!

1. The Tamaskan Dog Is Famous

This Dog Breed Is North Caroline State Football Team's Mascot

These wolf-like dogs are a very individual breed making them famous worldwide.

Tamaskan Dog

Over the past forty years, the Tamaskan dog has made its way into the mainstream media.

Since 2010 a Tamaskan dog named Wave became the live Mascot of the North Caroline State Football Team.

The Tamaskan can also often be seen in the music industry, for example in music videos for groups such as the Lucretia Choir.

A dog breed of many talents, they have been seen in theatre and on Broadway. In 2016, a Tamaskan dog named Luchta played the role of "The Wolf" in Arthur Miller's The Crucible.

They are often seen in media because of their wolf-like appearance, but also due to their highly trainable working dog nature.

These dogs were bred to be everyday working dogs, and consequently, they are incredibly trainable.

The Tamaskan dog breed has a natural curiosity when it comes to learning, and consequently it may be beneficial to use tools such as a clicker to encourage their learning.

It is also important to know that the Tamaskan are incredibly loyal dogs, and so punishment should never be used. Using positive reinforcement dog training with Tamaskan puppies is the best way to guarantee a healthy and happy relationship with your dog.

2. They Are Not A Purebred Dog

But Are Recognized In The Foundation Stock Service

Tamaskan Dog

Tamaskan Dog Sitting

As well as their wolf-like appearance, the Tamaskan is known for its perfect personality.

Although the Tamaskan is a unique breed, it is not considered a purebred dog. Due to its easily traced pedigree (i.e. the crossbreed heritage), Tamaskans are often considered to be crossbreeds (i.e. hybrids).

Consequently, Tamaskans are not recognized by:

- The Fédération Cynologique Internationale
- International Kennel Club
- The Kennel Club (UK)

However, the Tamaskan dog is recognized by the American Rare Breed Association and is a member of the American Kennel Club Foundation Stock Service.

Since 2006, the Tamaskan has had its own breed club; the Tamaskan Dog Register (an international breed club).

The site acts as an international database for the Tamaskan dog breed, issuing registration paperwork and allowing Tamaskan owners to be matched with breeders near them.

Despite the fact that Tamaskan puppies cannot be sold as kennel club registered, this doesn't stop dog breeders from giving them premium prices, selling between $600 to $800 USD per puppy (with a litter size of between 6-10 Tamaskan puppies).

If you would prefer to rescue a Tamaskan dog as opposed to adopting, you may struggle to find one of these dogs in your local shelter!

It may be a good idea to check specialized breed pages, such as Tamaskan Rescue (a community page that rescues these dogs all around the world)!

3. Tamaskans Look Menacing

But Are Very Friendly & Affectionate

Tamaskan Dog

Tamaskan puppies love to play, it's a great way for them to learn social skills as well as exercise their brain and bodies.

Despite the fact that the breed is not aggressive, their looks, like a wolf, may be a perfect deterrent for anyone looking to make trouble, although they are more likely to be killed with kisses than anything else!

The Tamaskan may look like a fierce and angry wolf, but this dog breed is known to be a kind, loyal and affectionate good family dog.

Being excellent with children (playing gently and having great patience) Tamaskans are highly social dogs, and love to be at one with the family, rather than be left alone.

Due to their loyal and devoted nature, they can suffer from severe separation anxiety when left alone for long periods. This can be combatted by encouraging them, as Tamaskan puppies to be self-sufficient.

Beyond this, the Tamaskan is very intelligent and consequently does not do well with being bored. Being bred to work, with some of the world's most intelligent dogs as ancestors (i.e. Huskies), makes a Tamaskan for one very bored dog if left unstimulated for long periods! Left even longer alone, and there is a serious risk of separation anxiety.

The Tamaskan can be aloof with strangers and may take a while to come around.

This can be aided with socialization as a puppy, your Tamaskan to as many people and places as possible while young can make for a motivated adult dog.

However, do not let the less desirable qualities of the Tamaskan dog put you off...

They love to be by their owner's side, and their larger size and wolf-like appearance do not dissuade them from being lapdogs.

Enjoying the serenity of the countryside and loving nothing more than a good romp in the outdoors, as befits their Siberian Husky and Czechoslovakian wolfdog linage, Tamaskans love a good walk!

4. The Tamaskan Is Incredibly Low Maintenance

When It Comes to Food and Grooming – This Dog Breed Is Easy

Head Portrait of Gray Tamaskan

Beyond their everyday working-dog exercise requirements (which are anything but low maintenance), the Tamaskan dog breed needs very little else.

Tamaskans do well on a variety of diets, including dry, wet and raw.

If you choose to feed dry or wet commercial food, the food must be age-appropriate (i.e. puppy, adult, or senior dog) so as to avoid health issues.

Owners may also wish to consider a brand specifically formulated for working dogs. It should also be grain-free and high quality, as dogs struggle to digest a lot of the complex carbohydrates found in low-quality dog foods.

When it comes to grooming requirements, the Tamaskan dog breed is incredibly low maintenance:

- Tamaskans shed twice yearly and will need brushing every other day during this time.
- For the rest of the year, a Tamaskan will need brushing once weekly, if that, and bathing only when they get muddy.

The Tamaskan dog's coat produces natural oils that clean the dog's black grey, red-grey, or wolf grey coat. These oils should not be interfered with through bathing. Doing so could lead to health issues.

It is also not necessary to clip this dog, the Tamaskan, meaning that they are relatively fuss-free!

The Tamaskan will on occasion need their nails trimmed if they are more inactive, but with their recommended activity level the dog should be able to wear down their own claws.

Remember that nail trimming of any dog breed should only be done by a qualified professional, such as a groomer or a veterinarian. The Tamaskan dog is no exception.

As for more serious health problems, degenerative myelopathy and hip dysplasia are possible with Tamaskans.

Without any such serious health problems, the average lifespan for a Tamaskan is 15 years.

Summary

The Tamaskan dog is a smart, loyal companion, perfect for an individual or a good family looking for a high-octane wolf-like working dog.

These fun-loving dogs are perfect for anyone looking for a hiking, swimming, or jogging buddy!

However, if you are not up for their weekly mileage, perhaps consider a lower maintenance wolfdog, such as a Husky Cross or a Miniature Husky. And don't forget that left alone for long periods, the Tamaskan dog breed can suffer from separation anxiety.

With patience, love (and a lot of exercise), the Tamaskan can thrive in the urban or city environment.

Do you have this dog breed at home? Thinking about getting a Tamaskan puppy? Or just a Tamaskan superfan! Leave us your thoughts on this breed in the comments.

Printed in Great Britain
by Amazon

83853444R00038